*Wedgwood reclining figure of 'Ariadne', about 1870.*

# PARIAN WARE

Dennis Barker

Shire Publications Ltd

## CONTENTS

Introduction .......................................... 3
Techniques of manufacture ................... 5
Victorian pioneers ................................. 9
The art unions ....................................... 11
Identifying the principal makes ........... 13
Places to visit ........................................ 32
Further reading ..................................... 32

Published in 1998 by Shire Publications Ltd, Cromwell House, Church Street, Princes Risborough, Buckinghamshire HP27 9AA, UK. Copyright © 1985 by Dennis Barker. First published 1985; reprinted 1998. Shire Album 142. ISBN 0 85263 737 3.
All rights reserved. No part of this publication may be reproduced or transmitted in any form or by any means, electronic or mechanical, including photocopy, recording, or any information storage and retrieval system, without permission in writing from the publishers.

Printed in Great Britain by CIT Printing Services, Press Buildings, Merlins Bridge, Haverfordwest, Pembrokeshire SA61 1XF.

British Library Cataloguing in Publication Data. Barker, Dennis. Parian ware. – (Shire albums; 142). 1. Parian porcelain. I. Title. 738.2'7    NK4399.P3. ISBN 0-85263-737-3

COVER: *A version of 'The Three Graces' in Parian, marked on the base (TT) 65.*

ACKNOWLEDGEMENTS
I would like to record my thanks for the help and advice I have received from many quarters, including some of those listed under 'Places to visit' and some of the authors of books listed under 'Further reading'. Mr Robert Copeland of the original Copeland family, Historical Consultant to the present-day Spode company, was especially helpful; I am also indebted to Mrs Lynn Miller, Museum Information Officer, Wedgwood Museum; Mrs Joan Jones, Curator of the Minton Museum; Mr H. E. Frost, Curator of the Dyson Perrins Museum; Mr Stephen O'Neill of the Belleek Pottery Ltd; and various members of the staff of the Metropolitan Museum of Art, New York. My thanks, also, to Miss Sarah Alwyn, who checked and typed the manuscript. Photographs on the following pages are acknowledged to: Belleek Pottery Ltd, 5, 12, 13, 14; the Dyson Perrins Museum, 26, 27 (right); the Metropolitan Museum of Art, New York (gift of Dr Charles W. Green, 1947), 29; the Minton Museum, Royal Doulton Tableware Ltd, 7 (lower), 8, 21, 22, 23 (upper); the Russell-Cotes Art Gallery and Museum, Bournemouth (photographed by Harold Morris), 4, 30 (left); the Spode Museum Collection, 7 (upper), 16, 17, 18; the Trustees of the Wedgwood Museum, 19, 25. Those on pages 3, 10, 19, 23 (lower), 28 and 31 (upper left) are from the author's collection; other illustrations are from various private collections.

*Ariadne, or Voluptuousness, height 260 mm, unmarked.*

LEFT: *Bust of the Duke of Wellington. Marked 'JOSh Pitts, Sc London 1862', no maker's mark. Height 230 mm.*
CENTRE: *Unmarked bust of Dickens. Height 235 mm.*
RIGHT: *Bust of William Thackeray. Robinson and Leadbeater, marked 'Thackery' (sic). Height 200 mm.*

# INTRODUCTION

Before the middle of the nineteenth century, the only people who could afford portrait busts and other pieces of sculpture in their homes were the rich, who could afford marble, and the upper middle classes, who could afford a brittle, chalky white porcelain imitation called biscuit.

The invention that made busts of Queen Victoria, Palmerston, Dickens and other contemporary personalities available to the owners of villas as well as mansions was Parian porcelain — lighter, more creamy in texture, more pleasing to the eye than biscuit, and less expensive.

It originated in the early part of Queen Victoria's reign (1837-1901), when the British Empire was at its peak, and was fashioned into objects of utility and ornament, such as decorative vases bearing Queen Victoria's head and match holders embodying ragged urchins. It was turned into portrait figures or busts of the men and women who were most influential in the Victorian and Edwardian era but it started to become coarsened and defunct at about the time of the First World War (1914-18), though examples — sometimes comparatively crude — were made up to the outbreak of the Second World War and beyond. The Belleek Pottery in Ireland still makes Parian of fine workmanship to traditional designs, but glazed.

It is necessary to define Parian, especially as cheap plaster figures and busts imitating it are now being made and are sometimes confused with the real thing. Parian is a porcelain imitation of marble from Mount Elias on Paros, a Greek island in the east of the Aegean Sea — the sort of marble used for the Elgin Marbles in the British Museum. It is a porcelain of smooth surface, usually matt and almost always unrelievedly ivory in colour. Pieces which survive are almost all in the shape of figures, busts or intricate groups of figures and animals. Vases, jugs, medallions, spill holders and sundry ornaments were made at the time and are still to be found, though most were probably thrown away. Parian originated in Britain, and most Parian continued to come from Britain throughout its three quarters of a century of production, though some American and continental Parian was made.

ABOVE: *Figure group, 'L'Accordee de Village', French, unmarked. Height 240 mm, about 1860.*

LEFT: *Group depicting 'Europa'. Unmarked, but attributed to Vienna. Height 190 mm, about 1860.*

*Present-day production of a Belleek cherub candelabra showing the progression of processes.*

# TECHNIQUES OF MANUFACTURE

Parian was a development of biscuit porcelain, a previous imitation of marble produced by first baking and then firing in an oven or kiln. Biscuit ware was produced extensively in France (Sevres) and elsewhere in the nineteenth century. It was produced in England, mainly at the Derby works, which continued to manufacture it into the nineteenth century. Items in biscuit were usually thick-walled, heavy, dead white and granular in appearance. All these disadvantages were overcome in the later introduction of Parian ware.

At the time of its production items in biscuit were more costly than glazed and coloured items, because glaze and colouring could be used discreetly to conceal flaws in finish. The same applied to Parian from the time of its introduction, a fact responsible for the high quality of finish in most Parian ware, though some of the later examples, produced in great numbers (one pottery alone produced 460,000 pieces in one year) have the more 'dead' granular appearance found in biscuit. Parian is normally silky in appearance and feel. Where biscuit is almost opaque, Parian is translucent, as can be demonstrated by shining a torch into the hollows of busts or inside jugs.

Parian is a kind of bisque porcelain in a highly vitrified form. Far more than biscuit, it allows for fine modelling, which enabled the makers to produce remarkably lifelike portrait busts of personalities of the period.

The basic compound used to make the porcelain was known as frit and consisted of a vitreous mixture of silica and alkali. It was ground, and white clay with lime was added. Especially at the beginning of the period of production, and for easier fusibility, the mixture used included a strong proportion of glass and ball clay, producing a rather 'transparent' look characteristic of Parian.

In general Parian differed from 'true'

porcelain in containing glass and in the proportions of its other constituents. Usually the proportion of the felspar of the china stone to the china clay was in two parts to one. However, the formula used throughout the heyday of Parian — roughly the Victorian and Edwardian periods — varied from company to company. Copeland and Garrett, who claim to have produced the first Parian, used frit composed of fifty-seven parts of white sand, eleven parts of Cornish stone and eight of potash. The Parian itself was composed of twenty-four parts of frit to thirty-six parts of china clay and forty parts of felspar. The firm also produced a felspar porcelain marked 'Late Spode', a bridge between biscuit and Parian that resembles biscuit in its chalky appearance and heavy weight.

The amount of iron silicate present in the felspar generally used at the time affected the final colour of the Parian. The more iron silicate there was in the felspar, the more creamy the texture as distinct from pure white. The mixture, whatever its constituents, was mixed with water until it had the consistency of rich cream and was then poured into moulds made of plaster of Paris.

The fineness of the finished model depended greatly on two things: the skill of the mouldmaker and, perhaps even more important, the skill of the maker of the miniature copy of the statue to be reproduced — or the original work of art, created specifically for the purpose, be it a portrait bust, jug, dish or allegorical group of figures.

It was usual to reduce larger portrait busts by the use of an invention by the sculptor Benjamin Cheverton, who patented it in 1844. It is now in the Science Museum in South Kensington, London. Called a 'three-dimensional pantograph', it consists of a frame built on the scissors principle. One end was moved over the outline of the large bust to be copied, while at the other end of the device a pointed marker drew the bust, but in reduced size.

The resultant model (for which alabaster was used more than wax because of its greater durability) was passed on to a block cutter. He would cut the model into pieces from which it was possible to make moulds. According to Charles and Dorrie Shinn in their comprehensive book *Victorian Parian China*, one of Copeland and Garrett's groups of seven figures, called 'The Return from the Vintage', had to be split up into over fifty moulds before it was possible to create pieces which could successfully be moulded and fired.

The moulds were then created from these pieces of the model, usually using plaster of Paris. The slip was then poured into these moulds, which allowed the moisture to dry out into the plaster. The reason that Parian is almost always much thinner, lighter and more attractive than the older, press-moulded biscuit is that, as the special slip progressively coated the inside of the mould, the process could be stopped when a thin but adequately strong thickness had been achieved.

After this, the pieces were passed on to a workman misleadingly called the repairer. His job was to reconstitute the pieces into a whole figure, object or group. He had to take special care when working the joints. If they started coming apart they might have to be repaired with more slip, which had to be part of the same consignment used for the original work. Parian figures shrank considerably in firing and a different shrinkage rate in the joints would have ruined the piece. Those parts of the figure liable to collapse had to be supported by props with powdered flint on the end to prevent them adhering to the figure.

After being left in a warm room for about a week to dry thoroughly, the figure was put into the firing kiln for sixty hours at a maximum temperature of 1060 to 1100 degrees Celsius. Then it was allowed to cool gently and the seams were rubbed down until absolutely smooth before it was put back for its second firing at an even higher temperature. This produced, by vitrification, the smooth creamy surface of the Parian, which is its most recognisable characteristic.

The fact that the piece continued to shrink during all firings — occasionally there were three or more — was a bonus, not a disadvantage. As when a drawing or photograph is shrunk for its appearance in a book or newspaper, the definition of the piece became sharper and clearer the

ABOVE, LEFT: *Copeland figure, 'Shepherd Boy', after L. A. Malempre. 1871. Height 445 mm.*
CENTRE: *Copeland figure, 'Egeria', after E. H. Foley. Coloured with touches of gilding on bangles and drape. 1894. Height 565 mm.* RIGHT: *Copeland figure, 'Musidora', after W. Theed. 1857. Height 425 mm.*
BELOW: *Minton 'inkstand — Chinese', celadon and white glazed Parian with 1869 year cipher. Height 180 mm.*

smaller it became, providing it had been crisply shaped. It is said that some pieces of Parian shrank by as much as a quarter. The precise modelling — especially of human faces, with their perfectly formed features and wrinkles — is one of the features of Parian that delighted at the time the items were produced and continues to delight. However, the process was not cheap and large Parian pieces went only into prosperous households.

*Minton Parian group, 'John Anderson, My Joe', with year cipher for 1867. Height 250 mm.*

*Three Wedgwood Parian figures: possibly 'Broken Heart' by E. Shenton; 'Faun with Infant Bacchus'; and bust of Shakespeare.*

## VICTORIAN PIONEERS

There is a dispute about who found Parian first, and also about who first manufactured it commercially. One of the foremost authorities on the subject was Llewellyn Jewitt, who became vice-president of the Derbyshire Archaeological and Natural History Society and was a member of the Russian Imperial Archaeological Commission and of the Numismatic and Antiquarian Society of Philadelphia. In his classic book, *The Ceramic Art of Great Britain*, first published in 1878 and republished at least twice later, he asserted that Parian had been contrived at the suggestion of John Gibson, an English sculptor who spent most of his life in Rome.

Gibson came back to England in 1844, when experiments on what later came to be known as Parian were being carried out by more than one Staffordshire china firm in an attempt to find a cheaper, lighter, more pleasant substitute for white marble than Derby biscuit porcelain. He spoke to Sir Robert Peel, the Prime Minister, about the state of sculpture in Great Britain and about the possibility of sending young sculptors to Rome to study. The new white compound was discussed at the same time. Gibson was certainly one of the first men who were both aware of the new possibilities of Parian and influential enough to speed its progress; but Jewitt's firm claim that Gibson initiated the invention has been disputed.

Thomas Boote claimed to have first made Parian in 1841. Three men connected with Copeland and Garrett have been variously credited with first producing it: Spencer Garrett, one of the partners; Thomas Battam, the art director, and John Mountford, one of the firm's employees. Mountford's claim to have discovered the formula first is a strong one, though the discovery and development could have been partly accidental.

Mountford had been apprenticed at

the Derby works, where biscuit figures were made from the 1770s. He went to Copeland and Garrett to start the figure trade there. Experiments were conducted to find the secret of the Derby biscuit formula, because Derby biscuit was less starkly and chalkily white than the Minton biscuit of the same period. It was in the course of these experiments that someone, probably Mountford, discovered a substance different from biscuit and more congenial. It was at first known as statuary porcelain, then specifically as Parian.

The honour of being the first *manufacturer* of Parian, once it was discovered, is also in dispute. Three firms — Copeland and Garrett (formerly Spode, the name it reassumed in 1970), Minton and T. and R. Boote — all laid claim to the distinction, though none of them has been able to prove its claim beyond dispute.

ABOVE, LEFT: *Minton bust of Colonel Colin MacDonald, after Minton design 490. Height 240 mm.* CENTRE: *Benjamin Disraeli, Lord Beaconsfield, with impressed mark, 'Beaconsfield, Protected Act 54 George III. L. G. & Co. 9/9/78 L. A. Malempre. COPELAND'. Height 295 mm.* RIGHT: *Sir Robert Peel. A fine Copeland specimen from a sculpture by James Westmacott with impressed mark, 'James Westmacott, sculpt. published August 18th 1850'.*

BELOW, LEFT: *Bust of Milton in felspar porcelain, a cream porcelain which preceded Parian. Marked 'Copeland & Garrett (late Spode)'. Height 190 mm.* CENTRE: *John Bright, the reformer. Robinson and Leadbeater. Height 165 mm.* RIGHT: *This bust of Wagner, 205 mm high, is of white plaster. Plaster busts are solid and easily distinguished from hollow Parian ware.*

*Three Wedgwood Parian figures. They depict 'England', modelled by William Beattie, published 1859; 'Finding of Moses', also by Beattie; and 'Christ on the Mount'.*

# THE ART UNIONS

The popularity of Parian was greatly encouraged because of a social and artistic development of the Victorians called the Art Union movement. The invention of Parian came just after the formation in 1836 of the first Art Union, the objective of which was to 'advance art by the improvement of public taste and to advance civilisation by the improvement of art'.

A lottery was the basis of the Art Union idea. The prizes were of an artistic nature. By 1847, the proceeds of the lottery were £17,871. Winners were given money with which to make a purchase from selected exhibitions. At these, the objects were displayed before being taken home by the winners. The Union commissioned original works, beginning with engravings. In 1845 it announced it had 'determined to reduce some fine statues to a convenient size and to issue a certain number of copies in stone china, as manufactured by Messrs Copeland and Garrett'.

The fad blossomed in the display at the Manchester Exhibition of 1845. The Copeland and Garrett stand included a copy of the equestrian statue of Philibert, the model of 'Apollo as the Shepherd Boy of Admetus', and a 30 inch (760 mm) high lead-lined vase, copied from one in the British Museum. All were praised by the writers of the time.

Parian was obviously a product that could become the centrepiece of Art Union activities. It received a boost when John Gibson agreed to the reproduction of one of his noted works executed in marble. The statue was 'Narcissus': a version of it had been submitted to the Royal Academy as a diploma work in 1838. Later 878 copies of 'Clytie' ('The figure represented as if rising from a bud of the lotus', said the *Art Journal*) were given to people who had bought tickets for a decade without winning anything. This figure was reduced by C. Delpech in 1855 from a Roman marble bust in the British Museum, later identified as 'Antonia'.

*Belleek figure described as 'Erin Rises from her Slumbers', a figure produced in matt and glazed Parian from the mid nineteenth century to the present-day.*

*A Belleek girl basket bearer of the 1980s, to a design used in Victorian times, shown (left) before and after firing (right).*

## IDENTIFYING THE PRINCIPAL MAKES

Identification of Parian pieces, not all of which are marked, will be helped by the possession of some knowledge of the industrial setting in which they were produced.

The manufacture of Parian china took place mainly in three locations: the Potteries (Stoke-on-Trent, Hanley, Burslem); Worcester; and Belleek in County Fermanagh, Northern Ireland. Some examples were made at Derby, as a follow-on to the biscuit china made there in the eighteenth and early nineteenth centuries, but they were few in number. Other examples were made at Coalport, but these, too, were very few and are rarely seen today.

Parian was also made in other countries. In the United States, it largely featured American subjects, and the trade died out fairly rapidly. Germany was also active, but its Parian was often of a cruder and cheaper variety.

In the Potteries, the number of firms producing Parian was large in Victorian times, but only a handful of these are of much concern to collectors today. Such major makers and the means of identifying their wares are listed in this chapter, but the list does not cover all the Parian produced at the time, and items made by other firms are by no means to be rejected as of no interest. Some were fine specimens of the Parian maker's art.

The Keeper of Ceramics at the Victoria and Albert Museum, London, has been able to identify many collectors' pieces authoritatively, and there is an arrangement whereby, at certain times, experts at the National Portrait Gallery, London, will try to identify the *subjects* of busts and figures, though they have no special expertise in Parian ware as such.

In the case of American examples, the Metropolitan Museum of Art, New York, can be informative. But it was firms in the British Isles whose products dominated the market of their time and still predominate today.

The principal firms are discussed in alphabetical order.

*Belleek-covered oval basket showing the fine tracery work for which they have always been noted. Traditional design still in manufacture.*

## BELLEEK

The Belleek factory was founded in County Fermanagh in 1863, the year when the end of slavery was proclaimed in the United States (an event depicted by some makers in Parian figures showing black slaves).

The suggestion that the Belleek factory be set up came from John Bloomfield, who wished to exploit the considerable quantities of felspar and china clay under his land in the area. In April 1856, in *The Times* newspaper, Bloomfield advertised 'A bed of porcelain clay and felspar'. The variety of felspar available in Ireland produced the crystalline, sugary appearance characteristic of Belleek.

Originally known as McBirney and Armstrong, the Belleek firm became D. McBirney and Company. It was a partnership of Bloomfield, David McBirney, owner of a Dublin store, and R. W. Armstrong, the art director. It specialised in both soft-paste Parian (producing a creamy, smooth surface) and in hard Parian, which had a surface not only harder to the touch but also more 'gritty', which meant that it more easily collected dust. To cure this disadvantage, Belleek brought into use a form of lustre glaze invented by Jules Brianchon in 1857. This incorporated resin, bismuth nitrate and lavender oil and could be varied to produce anything from a slightly shiny white surface to a mother-of-pearl effect.

Numbers of lustre-glazed Parian figures, some quite large, were made by Belleek, including 'The Prisoner of Love', a woman naked to the waist with doves at her feet, at 25½ inches (648 mm) tall, the largest statuette made at the factory, and 'Hibernia Awakening from her Slumber', 20 inches (508 mm) tall and modelled by Gallimore, who was brought in from Stoke-on-Trent to help launch Parian production in Ireland.

Portrait busts included those of Charles Stewart Parnell, the Irish political leader whose effectiveness was broken by Gladstone and a divorce case, Wesley, Shakespeare and Dickens. Statuettes of 'characters' were also produced. Among these were 'Cavalier', 'Roundhead' and 'The Belgian Hawkers'. Figure candlesticks were made of an old 'Welshman' and 'Welsh Woman' carrying baskets.

But it was not in the production of busts and figures that Belleek was at its most characteristic. Large numbers of glazed open work baskets were made at the works. (They are still being made). These were decorated with hand-modelled floral designs, a speciality being the incorporation of the national emblems — the rose for England, the shamrock for Ireland, and the thistle for Scotland.

If one wishes to see the very best work of which the Belleek factory was capable in the past, one must go to museums. At the apex of their achievement was the icepail made for the then Prince of Wales. Its base was formed of three mermaids. These supported the base of the vase, formed like a shell, around which a group of Tritons and dolphins in high relief sported in the water. There was some colouring and gilding. Belleek's emphasis on marine life for its subject matter can be enjoyed in less ambitious forms. The works used more marine life for its motifs than any other factory, including those for wares it produced in Parian.

A tall, pointed tower with a wolfhound on the left and a harp on the right is used to mark early pieces of Belleek porcelain, with the work *BELLEEK* underneath. After about 1891 the words *CO. FERMANAGH IRELAND* were added. The firm, now known as Belleek Pottery Ltd, is still in operation, sometimes producing copies of work made in the Victorian period. It is regrettable that portrait busts do not feature in its present-day lists, since its Victorian examples were so fine.

## COPELAND AND GARRETT

Perhaps because Copeland and Garrett never made the sort of mass-produced and inexpensive crested holiday souvenirs that were produced in their thousands by firms such as Goss, the name of this firm and its later title of Copeland are not so immediately familiar to the inexperienced collector of Parian, but they are of supreme importance to the serious student of Parian ware.

The firm did not produce the very small portrait busts produced by Goss, Robinson and Leadbeater and other firms. Most of its busts were 9 inches (230 mm) tall at least, some of them much larger. Classical figures rose to well above 20 inches (500 mm). (Copeland busts were made principally for display on columns rather than on the average mantelpiece.)

The rich creamy texture characteristic of the firm's goods is one of the most attractive available in Parian and with practice is fairly easily differentiated from the harder white or bluish tint of other leading firms of the period.

Two of the commonest busts made under this imprint are of the Prince of Wales, after the statue by Marshall Wood, as modelled by F. M. Miller and 12½ inches (317 mm) high, and of Princess Alexandra, also modelled by Miller. Both often bear the impression *Crystal Palace Art Union*. Busts of Benjamin Disraeli, later Lord Beaconsfield, by Copeland, are rather more rare.

Rarer still are busts made by the firm in limited editions to commemorate political or social events. Sometimes these figures are representational and easy to recognise; sometimes they are of a more abstract nature, designed to appeal to an emotion as much as to deal in a direct image. One such example is the 9 inch (229 mm) tall head of a Negro slave, published in 1864. The slave has a chain around his neck. Inset into the rectangular plinth, fired as part of the figure itself, is a much smaller model of a reclining slave in chains. There is no description of the subject on the figure, which is now very rare, only the simple impressed mark:

*Pub May 1, 1864*
*COPELAND*

As the piece was published the year after the abolition of slavery was proclaimed in the United States, it could have been an edition principally for sale in America, whose own Parian manufacturers did not achieve the market dominance exercised by the British.

Classical figures produced by the firm over the years are of great intricacy, especially those modelled after Rafaelle Monti, like 'Night', a baby being watched

ABOVE, LEFT: *Copeland, 'Cupid Captive', after William Calder Marshall. Coloured with gilded bangles. 1884, Height 495 mm.*
ABOVE, RIGHT: *Copeland figure of Venus after John Gibson, known as the 'Tinted Venus'. About 1914. (The statuette was first exhibited at the 1851 Great Exhibition.) Height 420 mm.*
FACING PAGE: *Copeland, 'Infancy of Jupiter', after Raphael Monti. 1878 (sculpted originally 1871). Height 475 mm.*

over by a woman in swirling and apparently translucent cloak and veil, a remarkable trick of Parian craftsmanship.

The Copeland and Garrett company emerged from the original firm of Spode, which was established by Josiah Spode in 1770 and which made its reputation as an innovator in the trade by producing the first bone china within three decades of its foundation. In 1833 William Taylor Copeland acquired the business in partnership with Thomas Garrett. The partnership ended in 1847. Thereafter Copeland went on producing very fine Parian on his own. The firm arranged an exhibition of its own work on its London premises in 1859, including Parian busts of the same size as the original marbles. Some of the smaller ones were made by means of the reducing machine invented by Cheverton.

Because the partnership between Copeland and Garrett was almost over when the firm began to produce Parian, examples of the firm's work bearing the mark *Copeland and Garrett* are extremely

*Page from Copeland catalogue, about 1900 showing (from top, left to right) figures in various sizes: Love; The River Side; The Sisters; New Friends; Love; Studies from Life; Clytie; Studies from Life; Prosperity; Beatrice; Patience; Maidenhood; Adversity. The Beatrice is by Edward Papworth Junior.*

rare. Most of the firm's Parian busts and figures that will be found today bear the simple mark *COPELAND*, impressed on the back of the bust or on the back of the base.

Occasionally more information is given around the name mark itself, sometimes including the date, the name of the modeller, the subject of the bust and details of how copyright was protected. A portrait bust of Lord Beaconsfield also bears the additional information *L.G. & CO. 9/9/78*. W. T. Copeland and Sons, who are still in business today under the original name of Spode, say that the *L.G. & CO.* almost certainly referred to a specific retailer for whom a special order of the busts had been made, this being the frequent practice of Copelands at that period. This bust was originally sculpted by L. A. Malempre, a fact which is also impressed on the back.

Because Copeland used several modellers, the style of their busts is not immediately recognisable as, for instance, it is with Robinson and Leadbeater busts. But identification is easy because of the simple and clear markings usually employed, because of the texture of the material, and because, with the possible exception of Goss, Copeland wares were the most frequently marked.

In its subject matter, the firm of Copeland and Garrett began chiefly with allegorical figures and then swung towards realism. The Parian models produced by the company when it was under the Copeland and Garrett partnership, and covering the years 1842 to 1847, were mostly of such subjects as 'Apollo as the Shepherd Boy of Admetus', modelled from the statue by R. J. Wyatt for the Duke of Sutherland, who possessed the original. There was also a bust of a young girl, 'Psyche'; 'Paul and Virginia', after Cumberworth, a young boy and girl looking touchingly innocent; and 'Narcissus', the model from the John Gibson statue which was taken up so successfully by the Art Union of London.

Realistic figures of this period included a copy of Baron Marochetti's figure of Emmanuel Philibert, Duke of Savoy, on a horse; Lady Clementina Villiers, reduced by Benjamin Cheverton from the work by MacDonald; the Count D'Orsay's Emperor Nicholas of Russia; and the inevitable William Shakespeare.

The firm of W. T. Copeland, operating from 1847, produced a great variety of figures and busts, some allegorical, some realistic.

## W. H. GOSS

William Henry Goss came late to the production of Parian; he never displaced the august reputation of Copeland but in some ways refined and improved the art of manufacture.

Goss Parian busts and figures are excellently modelled. The eyes, in particular, have a life-like definition even in the smallest examples. The comparatively short period of their production adds to their rarity.

Goss was born in London in 1833. As a young man he worked in the Stoke-on-Trent factory of Copeland and Garrett. In 1858, he left to set up his own business in Stoke-on-Trent. It was not until 1865 that Goss began the production in quanti-

*Portrait bust of Sir Walter Scott, W. H. Goss (Falcon mark underneath base). Height 135 mm.*

ty of Parian busts and figures, nearly twenty years after Copeland and Garrett entered this field.

The subjects of Goss busts are similar to those made by the other distinguished firms — royalty, musicians, writers, statesmen, soldiers and other personalities of the period. Most copies were made in the 1870s and 1880s, but new models were being introduced until just before the First World War in 1914. According to John Galpin, a leading authority on Goss of all types, models of Sir Walter Scott and Napoleon continued in production until the 1930s. This explains why the Scott bust is easier to come across than most other examples of Goss portraiture.

According to the knowledgeable Jewitt, in the second edition of *The Ceramic Art of Great Britain*, 'In Parian, for which Mr Goss ranks deservedly high, busts, statuary (notably an exquisite group of Lady Godiva), vases, tazzas, scent jars, bread Platters, and many other ornamental goods, are made. Notably among these are admirable busts of our beloved Queen, the late Earl of Beaconsfield, of Mr Gladstone, of Lord Derby, of Mr S. C. Hall (prepared for myself), of Charles Swain, and that of myself, an engraving for which forms the frontispiece of the first edition of this work, for which it was expressly modelled in 1875.'

These busts, said Jewitt, like all the busts which 'the pure artistic genius and manipulative skill of Mr Goss have produced', were of the 'highest style of Art in point of pose and poetic treatment, and of the most careful finish in workmanship. As portrait busts they rank high above the average and are, indeed, perfect reproductions of the living originals. It is not often that this can be said of portrait busts, but it has been a particular study of Mr Goss, and in it he has succeeded admirably.'

Goss may be positively identified with ease. Examples are clearly marked in a number of ways.

The commonest mark is that of a bird, the Goshawk, with the name *W. H. Goss* below it, transfer-printed in black on the back or under the base of the piece. Goss claimed this mark was used 'continuously' from 1862. Before this date an impressed *W. H. Goss* mark was used. It has been claimed that the presence of the impressed mark automatically means the piece is an early example, but this is not necessarily so. Both impressed mark and Goshawk mark appear on some Goss busts, notably on the very small one of Shakespeare, in which two folios act as the plinth.

John Galpin in his book *Goss China* has listed over fifty subjects of Goss portrait busts. These have been confirmed by the Royal Doulton Group, which owns the Goss assets. They vary from Queen Victoria in mob cap (in five different sizes) to 'Little Red Riding Hood', from Garibaldi to 'The Devil Looking over Lincoln'.

## MINTON

Before the Parian era began in the 1840s, Minton was already making finely modelled portrait busts and figures. Some of these early models — in the flatter, chalky white biscuit porcelain — were afterwards reproduced in Parian, so that for a time similar busts were produced in both materials.

This makes precise dating of Minton portrait busts without reference to markings somewhat chancy. It is fortunate that, at least from 1842 onwards, Minton devised a system of coded markings which not only positively identify the piece as Minton, but also indicate the year of manufacture. Otherwise the principal guide to identification would be the slight sheen of Minton Parian, resembling a hoar frost.

The presence of colouring can also indicate, to the casual eye, possible manufacture by Minton. The firm experimented widely with colour and for the 1851 Great Exhibition displayed figures called 'The New Shepherd' and 'The New Shepherdess'. These were just under 7 inches (180 mm) tall. Today they are extremely rare.

The Minton factory itself goes back much further than 1842, when Mintons started date-coding their porcelain. Thomas Minton, the founder, was born in 1765 at Shrewsbury and apprenticed as an engraver to Thomas Turner at the Caughley china works at Broseley. The porce-

ABOVE, LEFT: *Minton Parian figure, 'Clorinda', modelled by John Bell in 1848. Height 345 mm.*
ABOVE, RIGHT: *Minton Parian figure of Colin Minton Campbell, a reduced model by T. Longmore of a statue by Sir Thomas Brock, which stands outside the Minton Factory in Stoke-on-Trent. It has an 1877 year cipher. Height 485 mm.*

lain business was a small and rather inbred one. Thomas Minton first engraved coppers from which patterns were made for pottery firms, including that of Josiah Spode, who founded the Spode works, which was later to become Copeland and Garrett. Then Minton began producing pottery on his own account in 1793.

From the 1830s, the firm produced white biscuit figures, including 'Red Riding Hood', Hannah More, Queen Victoria, Wilberforce, Queen Adelaide, Sir Robert Peel, William IV and 'Greenwich Pensioner'. The full list of these models is given in Geoffrey Godden's *Minton Pottery and Porcelain of the First Period, 1793-1850*.

Parian variations of these models began to appear in 1847, sometimes repro-

Minton year ciphers — impressed marks in use between 1842 and 1942 (from 1943 to 1968 the last two figures of the year were impressed).

ducing the fine imitation of lace which had been a characteristic of the biscuit examples. Real lace was dipped in bone china slip (liquid clay) and then fired. This made the china solid, while burning out all the traces of the original lace. Busts of 'Ophelia' and 'Cleopatra', dating from the earliest Minton Parian period, used this effect.

About 150 models were manufactured in both biscuit and Parian, ending at about the time 'Ophelia' and 'Cleopatra' were being produced. Minton records, which are still preserved, include five hundred different examples, ranging from 'Bacchus and Cupid', Lord Palmerston and Lord Derby, to Marie Antoinette and 'Christ and His Disciples'.

Some of the earliest models included 'John Anderson My Joe' (about 1848), 'Dorothea' (1849), 'The Greek Slave' (1850), 'Clorinda' (1850), 'Pandora' (1851), 'Psyche' (1851), 'Naomi and Her Daughters in Law' (1851), 'Guardian Angel' (1852), Sir Robert Peel (1852), 'Venus' (about 1860), 'Solitude', 'The Lion in Love' and Colin Minton Campbell.

The firm's lists have been collated by an archivist.

The Minton mark did *not* appear on the very first biscuit and Parian figures, busts and other articles. At some time after 1842, the bases of some Minton pieces had arrow shapes incised in them — scratched with an implement, as distinct from impressed with a die. This was the maker's mark. Sometimes also, from this date, the wares were initialled by the workman responsible and dated with the month and the year of manufacture: for example, *3/47* would denote manufacture in March 1847.

The earliest date ciphers, which made

the recognition of later Minton a straightforward matter, were brought in around 1842.

*MINTON* was the standard marking from about 1862 and eleven years later an S was added at the end to make it *MINTONS*.

The firm still operates today (as part of the Royal Doulton Group).

## ROBINSON AND LEADBEATER

Robinson and Leadbeater portrait busts have been under-estimated by students of ceramics and collectors. Perhaps one of the main reasons was that the firm specialised in Parian and so never achieved the enormous prestige of Copeland and Garrett or Minton in the general field of porcelain. Another reason may have been that the firm did not begin

RIGHT: *Minton figure, 'Miranda', designed and modelled by John Bell. Height 405 mm.*

BELOW, LEFT: *Bust of the Reverend C. H. Spurgeon by Robinson and Leadbeater. Marked 'published by the Rev. G. Dunnett, manufactured by Robinson & Leadbeater, Stoke-on-Trent, copyright J. A. Acton FECIT 1878'. Height 120 mm.*

BELOW, CENTRE: *Bust of Tennyson. Robinson and Leadbeater. Height 190 mm.*

BELOW, RIGHT: *Bust of General Gordon of Khartoum. Robinson and Leadbeater. Height 190 mm.*

operations until 1865, at least ten years after Parian came into production. This deprived it of an innovator's role. Also, the firm was still in production until 1924. Its later productions, therefore, cannot yet be thought of as antique, though they are nevertheless of interest to collectors.

The very specialisation of Robinson and Leadbeater gave an extra refinement to its Parian busts. Their stocklist ran to several hundred different subjects, and though the detail and execution do vary the general level of fidelity to the subject matter is very high.

In the 1878 edition of *The Ceramic Art of Great Britain,* Llewellyn Jewitt wrote: 'The operations of the firm are entirely confined to Parian, and in this they provide statuary groups and figures in large variety; statuettes and busts, both classical, portrait and imaginative; vases of endless form, variety and size; centrepieces and comports of elegant design; flower stands; brackets and pedestals; bouquet holders; trinket-caskets; cream-ewers; jugs, and a considerable variety of fancy articles.'

In Jewitt's view, by giving their constant and undivided attention to this one branch of ceramic art, 'Messrs Robinson and Leadbeater have succeeded in so improving it both in finesse and purity of body and tone of colour, as to render their productions of far higher than average merit. They have studied excellence of body, originality of design, and cleverness of workmanship, as before that of marketable cheapness . . .'

The earlier products of the firm — certainly those produced before Jewitt's observations in 1878 — bore no mark. They included many large and intricately designed pieces, including busts of 'Clytie', 22 inches (559 mm) high, and of W. E. Gladstone, MP. At some time after this date, Robinson and Leadbeater adopted their typical *R & L* mark, sometimes impressed within a frame like an oval with the ends squared off, sometimes within a plain rectangle; and they also brought more standardisation to their designs.

The most commonly encountered Robinson and Leadbeater busts today are of one broad type and are easily identified. They are between 7 and 9 inches (178-229 mm) tall, more rarely 5 to 6 inches (127-152 mm), and stand on an integral square base with a recessed square neck between it and the bust itself.

There is another similarity that can be spotted. The people portrayed are many and varied but the actual modelling has a certain similarity. One man, Roland Morris, chief designer for the firm, eventually assumed responsibility for all designs, a fact which made for consistency at some cost of variety.

In texture, the busts are more like Copeland than Minton: they have a creamy, very fine, smooth matt surface which is most attractive and which feels 'soft' to the touch. The name of the person portrayed is usually impressed in the neck of the base, usually on the front but sometimes on the back.

In the 1870s, most of the firm's products went abroad, principally to the United States, whose Parian industry never seriously rivalled the British one despite the quality of some of its products. The firm produced busts of Abraham Lincoln, Charles Sumner and Governor Andrew.

Robinson and Leadbeater had two factories in Stoke-on-Trent, one in Glebe Street. This was originally founded in 1850 by Giovanni Meli, a modeller, who sold out to Robinson and Leadbeater in 1865. The second works, in Wharf Street, were begun in 1858 by Leveson Hill, but sold to Robinson and Leadbeater in 1870, after his death. After the double acquisition, the firm expanded rapidly.

## WEDGWOOD

Wedgwood evolved the delightful unglazed white china described as Carrara; the formula is so close to that of Parian that Carrara is usually classified as Parian.

Some of the portrait busts and groups made in Carrara were copies of items previously made in black basalt, a substance in which the firm makes busts and figures to the present day.

As a survival from the Victorian era, the most often seen Carrara bust by Wedgwood today is that of Stephenson, the engineer and pioneer of the steam locomotive. This was reduced from the

ABOVE, LEFT: *Statuary group 'Christ Healing the Blindman', Wedgwood.*
ABOVE, RIGHT: *Wedgwood figure probably depicting Diana (the huntress).*

work of E. W. Wyon and bears the name of the subject in *raised* letters on a simulated plaque at the front of the round base. There are also busts of, Shakespeare and Washington.

Most of the other subjects were classical. They included 'Ariadne', 'Charity', 'Cupid', 'Diana', 'Hercules', 'Infant Bacchus', 'Mercury', 'Morpheus', 'Triton' and 'Venus' — the usual range of Victorian subjects, all of them well wrought.

## WORCESTER

The term 'Worcester' as applied to Parian ware refers to the city, not to a particular factory, but it is generally used to describe the wares of Chamberlain and Company (previously Flight, Barr and Barr) and the firm which succeeded it in 1852, Kerr and Binns.

Marks of the latter firm include a crown enclosed within a double circle in which is printed *W. H. Kerr & Co* at the top and *Worcester* at the bottom. Some pieces of Parian also have marks incorporating the initials *K. & B.* or the words *W. H. Kerr & Co.* In 1862, the company became the Royal Porcelain Company. The present name is the Worcester Royal Porcelain Company Limited.

Most of the notable Worcester Parian items are not simple figures and busts, but elaborate and highly coloured items like tureens, salt holders and comports.

*Worcester comport, 380 mm high, modelled by Boyton Kirk. It formed part of the Shakespeare service produced for the Dublin Exhibition of 1853 by Kerr and Binns, forerunners of Worcester Royal Porcelain.*

Some of the early portrait busts are unmarked and detectable only because of the finesse of the workmanship and, sometimes, because of the shiny crystalline texture of the Parian. An instance is the abbreviated bust of Shakespeare on very simple lines (no wrinkles on the face, for example) but with a richness of surface which is immediately recognisable if the bust is put alongside more recently produced busts of the same subject that bear, for instance, the mark *H. Bros.* (The latter, in general design, resemble Robinson and Leadbeater, but they are usually smaller. They were made by Hewitt Brothers, of Longton, Stoke-on-Trent, from 1920 to 1926, and are now collectable.)

From 1852 most of the Worcester Parian may be recognised because of the similarities of its surface texture to that of Belleek.

MISCELLANEOUS MAKES

In addition to the renowned names already mentioned, there were many smaller manufacturers in the Potteries and elsewhere turning out Parian items of some interest in the Victorian period. Many of these did not mark their wares. Identification can therefore be difficult.

Several of the smaller and lesser firms made aesthetically pleasing examples that could pass as the work of the previously named firms. Among them were Samuel Alcock and Company, who are credited with producing in either biscuit or Parian

ABOVE, LEFT: *An unmarked figure representing 'Harvest-time'. Height 330 mm.*
ABOVE, RIGHT: *Worcester figure of King Lear, described as rare and originally retailing for 45 shillings, about 1865.*

a number of groups and allegorical figures and at least one figure of a real person, Fanny Ellsler, the dancer.

T. and R. Boote sprang in 1842 from the firm started by Joseph Machin and later carried on by his son William Machin and Partners, producing, among a wide variety of items, biscuit figures of well known people of the period.

The firm passed into the hands of T. and R. Boote in 1850, when Bootes were already well launched on their production of Parian. Bootes, who claimed to have originated Parian around 1841, produced a handsome bust of Sir Robert Peel after Sir Thomas Lawrence, statuettes of Shakespeare, Milton and Venus, and a number of allegorical groups and vases.

John Rose and Company, of Coalport, exhibited a clock case, a flower vase, a basket and a number of figures at the 1851 Great Exhibition. Their figures included those of the Duke of Wellington, seated, Queen Victoria, the Prince Consort, the Prince of Wales and Princess Alexandra. The pieces usually bore the name of the firm incised (cut) into the surface of the material or made part of a printed mark. The firm also used the word *Coalbrookdale*.

The firm today trades at Coalport, a division of Josiah Wedgwood and Sons

Limited, a member of the Wedgwood Group.

## CONTINENTAL EXAMPLES

Towards the end of the Victorian era some continental manufacturers began to make cheap, hard-paste Parian for the British market. The Germans especially were responsible for this initiative. In some cases models made in Britain were simply copied with modifications, no manufacturer's name being indicated.

## AMERICAN PARIAN

Parian was produced in America, beginning at much the same time as the first appearance of the British product, but production did not continue for so long.

Among the earliest makers in the United States were the potteries at Bennington, Vermont; but Parian was produced only from 1847 to 1858. Charles Cartlidge and Company, in Greenpoint, New York, started a year later — 1848 — and stopped two years earlier, in 1856, when the British industry was expanding following the impetus of the Great Exhibition of 1851. The pattern was repeated with numerous other firms.

An excellent illustration of the sort of item the American industry produced is provided by the collection of 5 to 7 inch (127-178 mm) portrait busts, probably Bennington, in the American Wing of the Metropolitan Museum of Art, New York. These represent American political figures such as George Washington, Mary Washington, Lafayette and also European subjects like Byron, Shakespeare and John Wesley.

The Metropolitan Museum of Art in New York has two items definitely identified as made by the US Pottery Company at Bennington. These are a 7 inch (178 mm) high syrup jug and a charming figure of 'Red Riding Hood' with a basket at her feet, 6¼ inches (159 mm) in height.

Much of the Bennington output was unmarked, like the double-sided portrait jug or spill holder of Charles Dickens. The Metropolitan Museum of Art has a number of Parian items which it describes as 'probably' Bennington. These include a 4 inch (107 mm) high model of Shakespeare's birthplace; a female figure with a basket of fruit called 'Autumn', 13⅛ inches (333 mm) high; a highly decorative and encrusted ewer 12 inches (305 mm) high; and a trinket box 6 inches (152 mm) long with doves in a nest with eggs on the lid.

The Metropolitan Museum of Art also has larger busts of Washington and Franklin, dating from a later period, the 1876 American Centennial Celebration. These were designed by Isaac Broome for the firm of Ott and Brewer, of Trenton, New Jersey. There is also a bust of General Grant from the New York City Pottery.

Collectors should also be aware of some of the early Parian and Belleek wares made at Trenton, New Jersey. In addition to Ott and Brewer (1873), who exhibited at the American Centennial Exposition (1876), there were the Willets Manufacturing Company, which made Belleek ware from about 1881; the Ceramic Art Company, formed in 1889 and which in 1906, under the guidance of Walter Scott Lenox, became Lenox Incorporated; and the American Art China Works, which also made Belleek ware. Today certain items produced by the

*A double-sided portrait vase or spill-holder of Dickens, unmarked but possibly made by the Bennington Potteries in the USA. Height 150 mm.*

RIGHT: *American Parian bust of George Washington. Mid nineteenth century, probably Bennington, Vermont. Height 170 mm.*

BELOW, LEFT: *American Parian model of Shakespeare's birthplace. Mid Nineteenth century, probably made at the Bennington works, Vermont. Height 100 mm.*

BELOW, RIGHT: *American Parian syrup jug, US Pottery Company, Bennington, Vermont.*

ABOVE, LEFT: *Cupid and Psyche, bearing the crossed shield mark of Dresden. Height 305 mm, about 1875.*
ABOVE, RIGHT: *An unmarked figure of a Roman lady, thought to be Diana, from an antique marble. Height 355 mm.*

Franklin Porcelain Company of Aston, Pennsylvania, are made in Parian.

### UNMARKED PARIAN

Where there is no marking of any sort, it is often virtually impossible to say with certainty where a Parian piece was manufactured. Unmarked pieces vary from those made by the noted firms to crude examples whose manufacturers were perhaps not keen to claim credit. Coarseness of texture and design often betray a modern imitation.

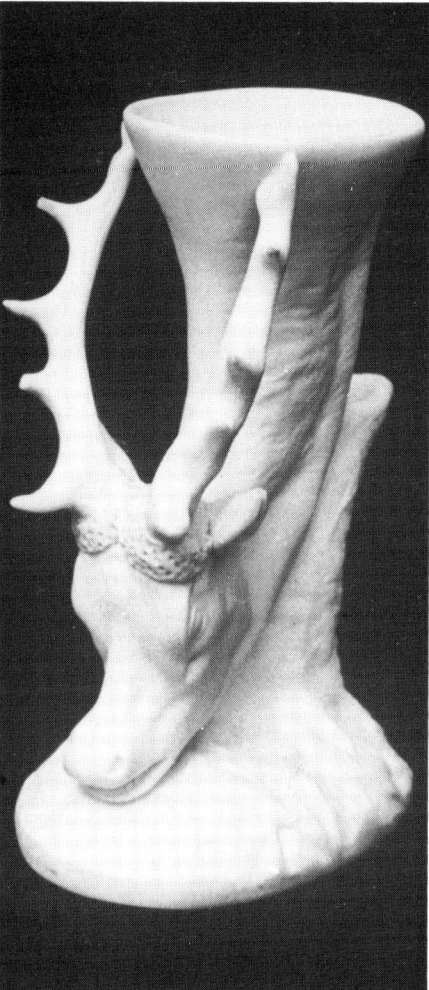

ABOVE: *Biscuit, full-length figure of Sir Robert Peel. Unmarked but almost certainly Minton. Height 270 mm.*

ABOVE, RIGHT: *Unmarked vase with glazed interior 'The Deer Head'. Height 145 mm.*

RIGHT: *Unmarked trinket or powder box with lid showing doves in relief.*

# PLACES TO VISIT

Visitors are advised to check opening times before travelling.

GREAT BRITAIN

*Minton Museum*, Royal Doulton Tableware Ltd, Minton House, London Road, Stoke-on-Trent, Staffordshire ST4 7QD. Telephone: 01782 292292. (Museum temporarily closed; telephone for information about reopening.)
*Museum of Worcester Porcelain*, Severn Street, Worcester WR1 2NE. Telephone: 01905 23221.
*National Portrait Gallery*, 2 St Martin's Place, London WC2H 0HE. Telephone: 0171-306 0055.
*Osborne House*, East Cowes, Isle of Wight PO32 6JY. Telephone: 01983 200022. English Heritage Victorian Collection in Queen Victoria's preserved holiday residence.
*Spode Museum*, Church Street, Stoke-on-Trent, Staffordshire ST4 1BX. Telephone: 01782 744011.
*Stoke-on-Trent City Museum and Art Gallery*, Broad Street, Hanley, Stoke-on-Trent, Staffordshire ST1 3DW. Telephone: 01782 232323.
*Victoria and Albert Museum*, Cromwell Road, South Kensington, London SW7 2RL. Telephone: 0171-938 8500.
*Wedgwood Museum*, Josiah Wedgwood & Sons Ltd, Barlaston, Stoke-on-Trent, Staffordshire ST12 9ES. Telephone: 01782 204141.
*Westminster Abbey*, London SW1P 3PA. Telephone: 0171-222 5152.

UNITED STATES OF AMERICA

*Cincinnati Art Museum*, Eden Park, Cincinnati, Ohio 455202. Telephone: 513-721-5204.
*Greenfield Village and Henry Ford Museum*, Oakwood Boulevard, Dearborn, Michigan 48121. Telephone: 313-271-1620.
*Metropolitan Museum of Art*, 5th Avenue and 82nd Street, New York, New York 10028. Telephone: 212-535-7710.

# FURTHER READING

Aldridge, Eileen. *Porcelain*. Paul Hamlyn, 1969.
*The Art Journal* of the Victorian period.
Copeland, Robert. *Wedgwood Ware*. Shire, 1995.
Copeland, Robert. *Spode*. Shire, 1998.
Dennis, Richard. *The Parian Phenomenon*. Published by the author, 1989.
Fisher, Stanley W. *A Start to Collecting English Pottery and Porcelain*. W. Foulsham, 1971.
Galpin, John. *Goss China*. Published by the author.
Godden, Geoffrey A. *The Handbook of British Pottery and Porcelain Marks*. Herbert Jenkins, 1968.
Godden, Geoffrey A. *Minton Pottery and Porcelain of the First Period, 1793-1850*. Herbert Jenkins, 1968.
Godden, Geoffrey A. (editor). *Staffordshire Porcelain*. Granada, 1983.
Gunnis, Rupert. *Dictionary of British Sculptors 1660-1851*. Abbey Library.
Hughes, Bernard and Therle. *The Collectors' Encyclopaedia of English Ceramics*. Abbey Library, 1968.
Jewitt, Llewellyn. *The Ceramic Art of Great Britain*. First edition, J. S. Virtue, 1878; second edition, J. S. Virtue, 1883; revised edition, Barrie & Jenkins, 1972.
Jones, Joan. *Minton*. Shire, second edition 1995.
Reynolds, Ernest. *Collecting Victorian Porcelain*. Arco Publications, 1966.
Sandon, Henry. *English Pottery and Porcelain*. John Gifford, 1969.
Sekers, David. *The Potteries*. Shire, 1981; reprinted 1998.
Shinn, Charles and Dorrie. *The Illustrated Guide to Victorian Parian China*. Barrie & Jenkins, 1971.
Wilkinson, Vega, *Copeland*. Shire, 1994.
Wills, Geoffrey. *English Pottery and Porcelain*. Guinness Signatures, 1969.